PRINCETON STUDIES IN INTERNATIONAL FINANCE NO. 18

Adjustment Costs and the
Distribution of New Reserves

Benjamin J. Cohen

INTERNATIONAL FINANCE SECTION
DEPARTMENT OF ECONOMICS
PRINCETON UNIVERSITY · 1966

PRINCETON STUDIES
IN INTERNATIONAL FINANCE

This is the eighteenth number in the series called PRINCETON STUDIES IN INTERNATIONAL FINANCE, published from time to time under the sponsorship of the International Finance Section of the Department of Economics at Princeton University.

The author, Benjamin J. Cohen, is Assistant Professor at Princeton University. Before coming to Princeton, he was an economist in the Research Department of the Federal Reserve Bank of New York. He has written a number of articles on the subject of international finance.

This series is chiefly intended to be restricted to meritorious research studies in the general field of international financial problems, both policy and theory, which are too long for the journals and too short to warrant publication as books.

While the Section sponsors the STUDIES, the writers are free to develop their topics as they will. Their ideas and treatment may or may not be shared by the editorial committee of the Section or the members of the Department.

FRITZ MACHLUP
Director

Princeton University
August 1966

PRINCETON STUDIES IN INTERNATIONAL FINANCE NO. 18

Adjustment Costs and the Distribution of New Reserves

Benjamin J. Cohen

INTERNATIONAL FINANCE SECTION

DEPARTMENT OF ECONOMICS

PRINCETON UNIVERSITY

PRINCETON, NEW JERSEY

Printed in the United States of America by Princeton University Press
at Princeton, New Jersey

CONTENTS

CHART

ADJUSTMENT COSTS AND THE DISTRIBUTION
OF NEW RESERVES

I. INTRODUCTION

The international debate on world monetary reform has entered a new phase. Previously, the discussion had focused on the issue first raised by such specialists as Robert Triffin[1]: is the creation of new international monetary reserves necessary? Now, however, a consensus appears to have developed that so long as the gold-exchange standard remains essentially unaltered, additional liquidity in fact will, sooner or later, be required.[2]

This is currently the attitude not only of national and international civil servants, but even of those economists in the academic world who would still prefer that reform move in the direction either of a modified gold standard or of greater exchange-rate flexibility rather than in the direction of extending the present system.

The issues now are more technical: how much additional liquidity does the system need, in what form should the new reserves be provided, and to whom should they be distributed?[3] In this essay I shall be concerned with this last question: the pattern of distribution. My purpose is to suggest—for reasons shortly to become clear—that whatever the amount and form of new reserves created, they ought to be distributed to countries in proportion roughly to the international distribution of the "transitional cost of balance-of-payments adjustment" (by which I mean the distribution of the cost of transition from international payments imbalance to an equilibrium with external balance).

First of all, this suggestion requires that we inquire into the determinants of the international distribution of transitional adjustment costs. The main argument in this study will be that the economic structure of each country has an important effect on its mode of adjustment required by external imbalance. That is, the international distribution of the transitional cost of adjustment is a function (at least partially) of the structural attributes of nations. Of course, it should be recognized from the start that this is a subject about which relatively

---

[1] Robert Triffin, *Gold and the Dollar Crisis* (New Haven: Yale University Press, 1960).

[2] See Pierre-Paul Schweitzer, "Fund Report at ECOSOC," February 24, 1966, reprinted in *International Financial News Survey*, Vol. XVIII (February 25, 1966), Supplement. But compare Emile Despres, Charles P. Kindleberger, and Walter S. Salant, "The Dollar and World Liquidity: A Minority View," *The Economist*, Vol. CCXVIII (February 5, 1966), pp. 526-529.

[3] See Schweitzer, *op. cit.*, p. 68.

few precise quantitative statements may be possible. Yet even an approximate, qualitative sort of insight would be extremely useful in working out the most suitable formula for distributing newly created reserves. For it is a fact that even while imbalances are by and large symmetrical and shared—one nation's deficit is another's surplus[4]— the cost of adjustment is not. Indeed, the process of adjustment normally proceeds quite asymmetrically, and the transitional cost of adjustment is frequently not even shared at all.

As we shall see, the heaviest burden of adjustment costs falls on the less developed countries, whose economies are particularly vulnerable to external pressures. And this makes for a strikingly "inequitable"[5] distribution, since it seems evident that these countries are compelled to pay a disproportionate share of the transitional cost of adjustment to disturbances wherever they originate, at home or elsewhere. Were they to receive a corresponding share of the new reserves to be created as a consequence of world monetary reform, the developing countries could employ their new resources to reduce their rather marked "adjustment vulnerability." In time, this would ensure that all countries share more equitably than they do now in the balance-of-payments adjustment process. True, distributing new reserves according to this pattern would deliberately link the problem of international liquidity and economic development. But that is precisely the purpose of this study: to indicate why this would be an appropriate procedure.

Chapter II of this study will discuss the meaning and significance of adjustment costs, and will suggest that in order to analyze the international distribution of transitional adjustment costs, it will be necessary to reconsider the role of the state in balance-of-payments theory. The proposed analytical model will be explored in greater detail in Chapter III. Chapter IV will consider the influence of four particularly important structural attributes of nations on the distribution of transitional adjustment costs. The study will end with a brief summary and conclusion.

[4] Ignoring special definitions of balance (such as the Lederer definition) and increases of monetary gold stocks, both of which have the effect of destroying accounting symmetry; and also ignoring statistical discrepancies, which may in some instances be quite substantial. See Poul Høst-Madsen, "Asymmetries Between Balance of Payments Surpluses and Deficits," *International Monetary Fund Staff Papers*, Vol. IX (July 1962), pp. 182-201.

[5] Tentative criteria of equity are proposed below in Chapter III.

Balance-of-Payments Adjustment

To explore the concept of adjustment cost, we must begin with the concept of adjustment. In accordance with standard practice, we may define balance-of-payments adjustment as "a marginal reallocation of productive resources and exchanges of goods and services under the influence of changes in relative prices, incomes, and exchange rates." This is the classical concept of "real" adjustment, the basic tool of balance-of-payments theory. Real adjustment is normally distinguished from transactions that merely finance an imbalance.[6] It is this concept of adjustment that will be employed in this study.

The nature of the adjustment process has been summarized most succinctly by Fritz Machlup's well-known Group of 32 Economists in its study of international monetary problems:

> The classical method of adjustment consists in a fall of money incomes, wage rates, costs, and prices in the deficit countries relative to those in the surplus countries. This can be brought about either by a change in exchange rates between the currencies of the countries concerned or by changes in the absolute levels of money incomes, wage rates, costs, and prices in some or all of the countries.[7]

In short, the process of balance-of-payments adjustment requires monetary inflation or currency revaluation by the surplus country or monetary deflation or currency devaluation by the deficit country (or some combination of the two).[8] This is so whether the imbalance of

[6] Lately, some dissatisfaction has been expressed regarding this conventional distinction. Under the pressure of the international-liquidity problem, economists have become acutely aware of how difficult it is to draw a line between transactions that require financing and transactions that perform the function of financing. This has led Fritz Machlup to propose an intermediate classification of "compensatory corrections," to describe transactions which help to "balance the accounts" (reducing the *need* for adjustment) but which do not themselves *constitute* "real" adjustment. See Fritz Machlup, "Real Adjustment, Compensatory Corrections, and Foreign Financing of Imbalances in International Payments," in Robert E. Baldwin *et al.*, *Trade, Growth, and the Balance of Payments* (Chicago: Rand McNally and Company, 1965), pp. 185-213. This contribution is useful, but it does not affect the definition of adjustment outlined in the text, since the new classification consists entirely of transactions that may be regarded as performing the function of financing.

[7] Fritz Machlup and Burton G. Malkiel (eds.), *International Monetary Arrangements: The Problem of Choice* (Princeton: International Finance Section, 1964), p. 25.

[8] For the sake of simplicity and clarity, I shall continue throughout most of this study to speak of payments imbalance as a matter involving just *two* countries, one in deficit and one in surplus. Although for most analytical purposes a two-

payments manifests itself initially as a "real" imbalance on current account or as a "financial" imbalance on capital account. Both are species of general disequilibrium; to achieve general equilibrium—and not merely some chimera of statistical balance—real adjustment is necessary.[9] That is, the deficit country must decrease its imports of goods and services from the surplus country relative to its exports of goods and services. And this can only come about through a relative realignment of money incomes and price levels in the two countries sufficient to generate the required reallocation of resources at the margin.

In fact, the balance-of-payments adjustment process has two dimensions: speed and magnitude. Adjustment may proceed swiftly or slowly; and the required resource reallocation may be moderate or extensive. It is manifest that these two dimensions are interdependent, though the nature of the interdependence is uncertain. On the one hand, it might be argued that for a given balance-of-payments disturbance, the longer the period over which the process of adjustment is stretched, the more resistant will be the untenable allocation of resources and exchanges, consequently the greater will be the magnitude and extent of the required reallocation. On the other hand, rapid adjustment or prompt initiation of adjustment may also involve rather extensive resource shifts, if it turns out that the disturbance was temporary and real allocation not called for.[10] I shall not dwell on this question of speed, since for our purposes this dimension of the adjustment process can be ignored. What concerns us more is the other dimension of adjustment: the magnitude of the marginal resource reallocation necessary to eliminate the disequilibrium. Indeed, this is the very sense of the classical concept of real adjustment, as I have already mentioned. The magnitude of the resource reallocation is, *ex ante*, the measure of adjustment required; *ex post*, it is the evidence that the process has taken place.

country model is sufficient, for some it is not. The most important limitations of the two-country model are noted and discussed in Chapter III, below.

[9] Real adjustment is hardly necessary in *all* situations of payments imbalance, of course. In certain conditions, where the disturbance is clearly temporary and non-repetitive—such as an earthquake or a crop failure—financing by means of gold and short-term capital movements is a much more appropriate response. But these are not the conditions that interest us here. In this study we are concerned only with disequilibrium situations of a more general and lasting nature; that is, situations where the payments imbalance is caused by persistent monetary inflation or deflation, or by permanent changes in the demand or supply schedules for particular commodities in international trade. In such situations, real adjustment is the only appropriate response. See Edward M. Bernstein, "Strategic Factors in Balance of Payments Adjustment," *International Monetary Fund Staff Papers*, Vol. V (August 1956), pp. 151-169.

[10] See, for example, Machlup and Malkiel, *op. cit.*, pp. 48-53.

It follows from what has just been said that *adjustment is a mutual process*, just as imbalance of payments is a mutual experience. For just as one country cannot be in deficit without a second being in surplus,[11] so resources cannot be reallocated within one of them without an equivalent and offsetting reallocation of resources within the other. In brief, the process of adjustment involves a reallocation of resources at the margin that is *complementary*. Should the deficit country, for instance, move resources that were previously employed in producing for the home market into export production, the surplus country will also find itself obliged to shift resources about as it begins to receive additional imports. Likewise, should the deficit country instead increase output in import-competing industries, the surplus country will find itself exporting less and therefore with additional resources available for use in production for its own internal market. In either event, the reallocation of resources is complementary; the process of adjustment is always *shared*.

However, while it is true that the *process* of adjustment is always shared, it is not true that the *cost* of adjustment is always shared. Quite the opposite is true, as we shall see. Furthermore, the process of adjustment is costly. Indeed, we may distinguish between two different costs inherent in the adjustment process, one a "transitional" cost, one a "continuing" cost.[12] The latter is never shared, and the former tends, more often than not, to fall on particular countries with certain specific structural attributes. In this study we shall be concerned primarily with the international distribution of the transitional cost of balance-of-payments adjustment. It will be useful, though, to begin with a brief discussion of the continuing cost of adjustment.

Continuing Cost of Adjustment

The continuing cost of balance-of-payments adjustment is *always* borne *wholly* by the deficit country. We have noted that real adjustment requires that the deficit country decrease its imports of goods and services relative to its exports of goods and services. This can be accomplished through (1) an absolute decline in the value of the debtor's imports with no corresponding change in the value of its exports (or with only a small rise of exports), (2) an absolute decline in the value of imports exceeding a corresponding decline in the value of exports, (3) an absolute rise in the value of exports with no corresponding change in the value of imports (or with only a small de-

[11] Again, we are ignoring special definitions, increases of monetary gold stocks, and statistical discrepancies, and speaking only in terms of a two-country model.

[12] I am indebted to Fritz Machlup for suggesting the terms "transitional cost" and "continuing cost," the meanings of which are much more readily apparent than those of the two terms I had originally intended to use.

5

cline in imports), or (4) an absolute rise in the value of exports exceeding a corresponding rise in the value of imports.

Associated with each of these four main alternatives is a very different combination of changes in real national income and real national "absorption"[13] in the deficit country: (1) a reduction of real national absorption of goods and services relative to a more or less stable real national income; (2) an absolute loss of national income as well as absorption (via unemployment or an unfavorable movement of the factor term of trade)[14]; (3) an increase of national income, all of which, however, is absorbed abroad; or (4) an absolute increase of absorption as well as national income.

Thus, it is clear that the approaches to adjustment are several in number. Yet the fact remains that in all cases the effect on the deficit nation is the same: its real national absorption is reduced relative to that of its trading partner. That is, at the new international equilibrium, the former deficit country must be worse off than the former surplus country, in the sense that it now receives a smaller proportion of the combined output of the two nations. This is the continuing cost of balance-of-payments adjustment. It is a continuing cost in that it is an open-ended phenomenon—the continuing real cost that the new international situation, *prevailing after all change has occurred*, imposes on the former deficit country. *Ex hypothesi*, this cost is at all times borne entirely by the deficit country, whatever the particular approach to adjustment.

To be sure, depending on the particular approach to adjustment, the *magnitude* of the continuing cost of adjustment required by any given payments imbalance may vary considerably. The magnitude of the cost, measured in terms of real national absorption foregone, is a direct function of the changes in real national income experienced in the two countries as a result of the adjustment process. Adjustment requires a reallocation of real resources, but similar resource reallocations can be generated by different adjustment techniques, and these different kinds of techniques may impose strikingly different costs in terms of human suffering and unpleasantness.

[13] See Sidney S. Alexander, "Effects of a Devaluation on a Trade Balance," *International Monetary Fund Staff Papers*, Volume II (April 1952), pp. 263-278. The expression real national "absorption" means the same as the term "domestic real intake," which Fritz Machlup prefers and which he defines as "the total domestic use for consumption and investment of goods and services valued at constant prices." See Machlup, "The Terms-of-Trade Effects of Devaluation Upon Real Income and the Balance of Trade," *Kyklos*, Vol. IX (1956), pp. 438-442.

[14] It should be noted that, in theory, there might be no loss of national income at all if a decline in the value of imports results entirely from a drastic movement of the net commodity terms of trade. Such a possibility is so unlikely, however, that we can safely disregard it as a practical alternative in this discussion.

In discussing different kinds of adjustment techniques, Staffan B. Linder distinguishes qualitatively between two major categories of reaction by deficit countries to external disequilibrium.[15] According to Linder, there are "negative" reactions, such as monetary deflation, trade restriction, exchange control, and currency devaluation[16]; and "positive" reactions, such as technological innovation or imitation and sales promotion. Although he does not explicitly say so, it is clear that corresponding to each of these two qualitative categories of reactions by the deficit country is a parallel category of reactions by the surplus country. Thus, following Linder, we may say that the surplus country reacts positively to external imbalance to the extent that it helps the deficit country avoid negative adjustment techniques—that is, to the extent that it inflates or revalues, or to the extent that it permits imitation of its technology or sales promotion in its home market. The surplus country reacts negatively to the extent that, by policies designed to preserve its payments position, it compels the deficit country to employ negative adjustment techniques.

It is no accident that Linder uses such normative terms as "positive" and "negative" to describe the reactions of deficit and (implicitly) surplus countries to mutual payments imbalances. Negative reactions tend to impose comparatively high continuing costs of adjustment on the deficit country in terms of real national income (and therefore absorption) foregone, especially insofar as they result either in an underemployment equilibrium or in protection to inefficient industries. Positive reactions, on the other hand, impose correspondingly smaller continuing costs, especially insofar as they result in improved technology, higher-quality products, or new market opportunities.[17] In short, the magnitude of the continuing cost of adjustment is a direct function of the kind of adjustment techniques employed. But the fact

[15] Staffan B. Linder, *An Essay on Trade and Transformation* (New York: Wiley and Company, 1961), p. 145.

[16] In reality, it is perhaps inappropriate to list devaluation unequivocally as a "negative" reaction; it might be more appropriate to list it in an intermediate "either-or" category, since in some respects—especially in respect of the transitional cost of adjustment—the effect of devaluation on the deficit country may be distinctly "positive." See below, the last section of this chapter.

[17] I should point out that, in adopting Linder's useful, but normative, terminology, I do not mean to introduce technical progress as a *deus ex machina* in balance-of-payments theory. I do not mean to imply, for instance, that a country *must* innovate or imitate because it has a payments deficit, or even that a country is likely to do so. On the contrary, I mean to imply only that there are different kinds of adjustment techniques, some of which are relatively high-cost, some relatively low-cost; and that among the latter we must, as a practical matter, include technical innovation and imitation. The terms "positive" and "negative" are used here to refer only to the magnitude of the cost implied by different kinds of adjustment techniques, not to the magnitude of their contribution to "progress" (however defined).

7

still remains that whatever the kind of techniques employed—positive or negative—the consequent continuing cost is borne entirely by the deficit country. At the new international equilibrium, it is always the former deficit country that receives a smaller share of the combined output of the two nations. With respect to this cost of adjustment, therefore, there is no problem of international distribution.

Transitional Cost of Adjustment

We have noted that the continuing cost of adjustment falls on the deficit country after all change has occurred, that is, after the process of adjustment is concluded. But the process itself also imposes a cost—the cost of making the change. Adjustment implies transition, a once-for-all phenomenon. And in economics each transition, each reallocation of resources, has its own cost, separate and quite distinct from the presumed cost of the new situation obtaining after the transition is complete. Thus the transition itself from payments imbalance to an equilibrium with external balance must also have a cost, separate and quite distinct from the continuing cost associated with the new international situation. This is the transitional cost of balance-of-payments adjustment.

Perhaps a simple illustration will help clarify the distinction being drawn here. Consider the individual worker who, having lost his job and being unable to find a comparable one, finally accepts a lower-paying position. This process of adjustment imposes two costs on the worker. The more obvious one is the real cost implied by the new position, that is, the difference between his previous wage and his new wage. This is an open-ended phenomenon, a loss of income that will continue so long as the worker remains in his new position. This, in other words, is the continuing cost for him of the adjustment process. But, in addition, the worker must have suffered some loss of income during his period of enforced idleness; there must have been some real cost involved in searching for a new job, possibly also the cost of moving his residence or investing in new skills. This is a once-for-all phenomenon, a single loss of income associated with the process of transition and change—in other words, the transitional cost of the adjustment process (which someone has to pay).

It is in this sense that we shall continue to speak of the transitional cost of balance-of-payments adjustment: to mean the cost of change, the cost of transition to the new international equilibrium. Unlike the continuing adjustment cost, which is measured in terms of real national *absorption* foregone and can therefore be expressed only *indirectly* as a function of changes in real national income, the transitional adjustment cost can be measured *directly* in terms of real national *income* foregone. Our problem is: how can we identify this cost, and how can we know who pays it?

Recall that the process of adjustment involves a relative realignment of money incomes and price levels in the two countries (deficit and surplus) sufficient to generate the required complementary reallocation of resources at the margin. This may be accomplished by monetary inflation or currency revaluation by the surplus country, or by monetary deflation or currency devaluation by the deficit country (or some combination). It is manifest that all of these alternatives are costly (though not equally costly): all imply that a certain amount of real national income will have to be foregone by one or both of the countries during the adjustment process—and because of it.

For example, some of these alternatives—monetary deflation, in particular—tend to result in temporary unemployment of a part of the national supply of manpower and machinery. Usually this may be expected to occur in the deficit country, but not necessarily—for instance, if the surplus country revalues its currency and as a result suffers a sudden and sharp loss of exports. Until such time as these idle resources can be reabsorbed into the production stream, the potential benefits from their productive capacity will be lost. Conversely, some of the four alternatives mentioned—especially monetary inflation—tend to result in a rising level of internal prices. This usually may be expected to occur in the surplus country, but once again not necessarily—for instance, if the deficit country devalues its currency without pursuing a sufficiently restrictive monetary policy. This result, too, may be costly. For, apart from their possibly unwanted effects on income distribution, accelerated price increases are apt to create an incentive for diverting investment resources from normal productive channels into such speculative activities as transactions in real estate and on the stock and commodity exchanges. Since this implies a certain distortion of the production structure, it means that the benefits of a more appropriate allocation of resources will be lost until such time as prices can once again be stabilized and the speculative fever has abated.

In practice, therefore, we may identify the transitional cost of adjustment—the amount of real national income foregone during and on account of the adjustment process—by observing the extent to which each of the two countries sharing a payments imbalance must undergo either price inflation or resource unemployment so that mutual balance can be restored.

Plainly, some part or even virtually all of the transitional adjustment cost may be borne by either country even though the adjustment process itself is shared. That is, the complementary reallocation of resources may be paid for largely or even wholly by either the deficit

9

or the surplus country. With respect to the transitional cost of adjustment, consequently, there does exist a problem of international distribution. This is the same problem that other economists touch on when they refer to the distribution of the "burden" of balance-of-payments adjustment.[18] Our concern in the remainder of this study will be with the question of who, in any case, must bear this "burden." Is balance restored (citing the most typical alternatives) via price inflation in the surplus country or via resource unemployment in the deficit country? In short, who pays the transitional cost of adjustment?

In the real world, of course, one country rarely pays the *entire* transitional cost of adjustment; in virtually all cases, the cost is in fact *shared* between deficit and surplus nations in some proportion. Most often, an accelerated price inflation in the surplus country is matched by a parallel demand deflation—or at least by a deceleration of the historic rate of monetary expansion—in the deficit country. Less frequently, but still significantly, adjustment may be accomplished by such a sharp rate of demand deflation in the deficit country that it causes price declines and unemployment in the surplus country as well, or by such a sharp rate of price inflation in the latter that it drags up prices in the former also. Only occasionally is it possible to identify a specific instance where all of the transitional cost of adjustment is borne entirely by one country. Even so, one may contend (for reasons to be discussed shortly) that in the majority of cases one of the two countries does tend to pay the overwhelmingly larger share of the cost of restoring mutual payments balance. Therefore, it probably does little harm to the facts of the matter to define the problem as if one of the two countries ordinarily bears virtually all of that cost.

Another point to be noted in this connection is that the transitional cost of adjustment, like the continuing cost, may in any given situation vary considerably in magnitude. In the first place, the cost associated with, say, price inflation—measured in terms of real national income foregone—is not likely to be the same in different countries, since national economic structures and monetary and fiscal systems may differ considerably. The same applies, of course, to the cost associated with demand deflation and resource unemployment. Moreover, with regard to any one country, the costs associated respectively with inflation and deflation are not likely to be the same or even similar. And, most significantly, in any one country the cost of either inflation or deflation alone can vary, depending on the kind of adjustment tech-

[18] See, for example, Tibor Scitovsky, *Requirements of an International Reserve System*, Essays in International Finance, No. 49 (Princeton: International Finance Section, 1965); and Robert A. Mundell, *The International Monetary System: Conflict and Reform* (Montreal: Private Planning Association of Canada, 1965), pp. 16-19.

niques employed by that country and by its trading partner in the process of restoring mutual payments balance.

In Linder's terminology, approaches to the adjustment process may be either positive or negative.[19] For example, in order to eliminate a payments imbalance in a particular circumstance, the deficit country may be obliged to undergo a certain amount of demand deflation. Associated with that deflation, however, there may be (to cite extreme alternatives) sheer, painful unemployment or an increase of productive efficiency resulting from technological innovation and imitation. In either event the deficit country pays all of the transitional cost of adjustment, but the magnitude of that cost varies depending on the kind of adjustment techniques employed by that country and by its trading partner. The same is true, of course, even in cases where some or even all of the transitional cost is paid by the surplus country. In all cases, the magnitude of the transitional cost of adjustment—like that of the continuing cost—is determined directly by the choice of techniques used in the adjustment process. And what determines the choice of techniques? I suggest that the basic explanation is to be found in the economic structure of nations.

A Reconsideration of the Role of the State in Theory

It is a fact of international economic life that the country paying the largest part of the transitional cost of adjustment—whatever its magnitude in the instance—need not be the same as the country that initiates the adjustment process. The policies of currency revaluation and devaluation are particularly important in this respect, since they are by definition substitutes for a direct realignment of internal money incomes and price levels. As such, they may serve to transfer the transitional adjustment cost from one country to another. Revaluation, for example, may enable the surplus country to avoid monetary expansion at home and, if successful, may even contribute to price inflation in the deficit country, though this effect is hardly inevitable. The more popular example is devaluation which, if successful, will almost certainly contribute to demand deflation and resource unemployment in the surplus country. Indeed, this is the classic example of a policy by which one country, in initiating the adjustment process, can transfer the bulk of the transitional cost to another. This in large part explains why currency devaluation (or depreciation) has always been regarded —especially in the interwar period—as such a handy weapon of economic warfare.

Other kinds of policies can also be used to achieve the same objective—namely, the transfer of the transitional cost of adjustment. These policies include trade restriction, exchange control, and sometimes,

[19] Linder, op. cit., p. 145.

11

under certain favorable conditions, even simple variations of interest rates. Such favorable conditions, for instance, tended to prevail for the United Kingdom during most of the nineteenth century, when London stood at the center of the international gold standard. Ordinarily, when a deficit in the British balance of payments threatened an outflow of gold from London, the Bank of England initiated the process of adjustment by raising Bank Rate. But this did not mean that Britain usually paid the transitional adjustment cost. Quite the opposite. Very often the cost was successfully transferred from the United Kingdom to the nations at the periphery—the primary producers of the Western Hemisphere and other outlying areas. For a tightening of credit in London tended to press especially heavily on the financing of trade in foodstuffs and raw materials, which were Britain's chief imports. Since this tended to force dealers to compress their inventories, correction of the imbalance was frequently accomplished not by monetary deflation or resource unemployment in the United Kingdom, but rather by a reduction in the prices and volume of British imports. Most of the transitional cost of adjustment, in other words, was borne not at the center but at the periphery, where exporting nations were compelled to deflate and, sometimes, to devalue.[20]

This distribution of the transitional adjustment cost tended to prevail regardless of the *origin* of the initial balance-of-payments disturbance. That is, whether the British deficit was due to an autonomous increase of demand at home or to an autonomous decrease of demand abroad, this same pattern of adjustment was likely to obtain. Furthermore, it was not only in the nineteenth century that a pattern such as this was likely to obtain; today, too, some countries are capable of transferring away from themselves the transitional cost of adjustment to disturbances originating internally as well as externally. This fact is important because it implies that a country capable of transferring the transitional adjustment cost by initiating the adjustment process is likely to be more tolerant of internally generated disturbances than a nation lacking such a capability. Hence it is likely to be a more serious source of instability in the international economic system.

Where a disturbance originates and whether the cost of adjusting to it can be transferred are matters of much importance in the context

[20] See Robert Triffin, "National Central Banking and the International Economy," *International Monetary Policies*, Postwar Economic Studies No. 7 (Washington, D.C.: Board of Governors of the Federal Reserve System, September 1947), reprinted in W. R. Allen and C. L. Allen (eds.), *Foreign Trade and Finance* (New York: Macmillan, 1959) Chapter 11; also Triffin, *The Evolution of the International Monetary System: Historical Reappraisal and Future Perspectives*, Princeton Studies in International Finance No. 12 (Princeton: International Finance Section, 1964), Chapter 1.

of our discussion. Indeed, they are crucial, for together they determine the kind of techniques that, in any given situation, surplus and deficit nations will employ in restoring balance. It is the choice of techniques, I have said, that fixes the magnitude of the transitional adjustment cost paid by each country. It is clear, therefore, that our subject requires that we consider two central and distinct (though interrelated) questions: (a) In which country does the initial payments disturbance originate?[21] (b) In which country is the process of adjustment initiated?

These are not idle academic questions. On the contrary, they represent a practical matter of considerable interest to all countries. Today, for instance, we are witness to a massive confrontation between the United States and the countries of continental Western Europe. Between them (and given the relationship of each with the rest of the world) there is a critical imbalance of payments. Although the two sides disagree as to where the disturbance originated, both agree that in the end, the United States, the deficit country, must bear the continuing cost of adjustment, in the sense that Americans must ultimately reduce their real absorption relative to national income. Yet neither side is willing to assume the responsibility for making the necessary accommodation; neither side, that is, wishes to pay the transitional cost of adjustment. The United States, fearful of unemployment, is loath to take deflationary measures and, because of the dollar's role as a reserve currency, refuses to devalue. Europe, meanwhile, is reluctant to countenance either monetary inflation or currency revaluation. Furthermore, neither side has been able to compel the other to pay the cost—in the fashion of Britain in the nineteenth century—by initiating the process of adjustment. And so the confrontation continues, with all of its potentially appalling implications for the international monetary system, and will continue until the two sides eventually work out—by accident or design—the distribution of the transitional adjustment cost.

To be sure, conventional international monetary theory tells us enough about how the transitional adjustment cost would be distributed between Europe and the United States if the adjustment process were allowed to operate automatically via price and income or exchange-rate changes. It would depend, more or less, on the combination of price and income elasticities and import propensities on the two sides of the Atlantic. But this is, in my opinion, insufficiently in-

[21] In the real world, of course, it is often difficult to identify the source of specific balance-of-payments disturbances. But this is an empirical problem, not a theoretical one. The fact is that disturbances must originate somewhere, and for the limited purposes of this brief study it is legitimate to proceed as if that "somewhere" can in fact be ascertained.

formative, for it fails to take explicit account of the fact that the United States and Europe are structurally quite different. America is a "giant among nations," the world's largest industrial and trading nation, the largest investor, and the largest dispenser of foreign aid. Europe, on the other hand, is a conglomerate of several countries, some more specialized in industry than the United States and some less so, some capital importers and some exporters, all smaller than the United States, some quite small. Should we not expect that the distribution of the transitional cost of restoring balance between America and, say, Germany will tend to differ from that between America and one of Germany's smaller neighbors, say Denmark or Austria (just as the distribution of the transitional adjustment cost between Britain and the continental European countries in the nineteenth century tended to differ from that between Britain and the nations of the periphery)?

This introduces a new dimension into balance-of-payments theory—the dimension of national economic structure—and requires a reconsideration of the role of the "state" in the monetary theory of international trade. Conventional analysis of payments imbalance and adjustment does not really take the state seriously. Like the positive (as contrasted with normative) pure theory of international trade, it is concerned principally with the competitive actions and reactions of large numbers of single, atomistic individuals and firms who, as it happens, can be classified into roughly homogeneous sub-groups by their nationality. The state as such has been given little importance beyond the fact that some of the participants in international trade and finance live and work there, obey its laws, and use its currency; the structural attributes of nations, such as size and level of economic development, are treated as largely extraneous.

In normative theory, to be sure, the state is taken much more seriously. Both in the theory of commercial policy and in international monetary theory when it is concerned with optimum payments policies, the state acts, both directly through government action and indirectly through governmental influence upon private behavior. Yet even at this level of analysis, insufficient attention is paid to the differences between states. To give just one example: conventional theory argues that when in deficit, a country ought, among other things, to raise interest rates in the hope of favorably influencing international capital flows. But surely, improvement of the capital account can be more easily achieved by lending less abroad than by borrowing more—that is, by a capital-exporting country rather than by one that imports capital. Likewise, improvement of the capital account can be more easily achieved by a nation where foreign participation in local financial markets is relatively extensive—that is, an international financial center—than by a nation where such participation is comparatively rare. The conventional theory, however, rarely makes systematic distinctions on these grounds.

Analytical distinctions of this kind based on differences of economic structure are probably needed. It may not be possible to make significant *a priori* statements in all cases, but an effort to do so would assuredly be worth while.

However, normative theory is not the principal interest of this study. Our concern here is with balance-of-payments theory in its positive aspects—in its attempts to predict the automatic processes of adjustment. The suggested new level of analysis is only slightly different from the conventional one; it is not in contradiction to it. At the new level of analysis, the conclusions of the conventional theory will be reinterpreted in the light of a differentiation between states based on their economic structure. In effect, the state itself will enter into the analysis *qua* state, not merely *qua* homogeneous grouping of private economic units. The behavior of atomistic competitors will no longer be considered independently of the characteristics of the national sub-groups to which they belong. Instead, their behavior will be analyzed as a function, at least in part, of the structural attributes of nations.

In effect, what I am proposing in this study is that we undertake to identify and analyze the determinants of one dimension of national *power* in international economic relations: the capacity to avoid the transitional cost of adjustment required by external imbalance. This capacity—or lack of it—is, as I have indicated, a practical matter of considerable interest to all countries. It ought to be of interest to economists as well.[22]

[22] In this connection, see Oskar Morgenstern, "Die Macht im Handel der Staaten: Ein Problem der Theorie des internationalen Handels," *Jahrbuch für Sozialwissenschaft* (1963), pp. 48-55.

Two Special Considerations

How can we analyze the distribution of the transitional cost of balance-of-payments adjustment? For the purposes of a short study such as this one, the analysis may be conducted on the level simply of formal verbal logic. What we must do is compare the capacity of different countries to avoid the transitional cost of adjustment required by any external imbalance, when the countries are differentiated (*ceteris paribus*) on the basis of individual structural attributes (to be specified in Chapter IV). For example, we might ask how the cost would be shared in the event of a bilateral imbalance of payments between two countries that are roughly comparable in all features except, say, "size."[23] Would a very small nation (let us call it Littleland) be compelled to pay all of the transitional cost of adjustment *vis-à-vis* a very large one (Bigland), or none of it? Two considerations demand special attention:

(1) *Would the answer differ according to which country is in payments deficit and which is in surplus?* This question is important because, as suggested earlier, the transitional costs of adjustment required by surplus and deficit are not likely to be identical even for any one country. Consequently, some countries are willing to tolerate monetary inflation more readily than deflation; others, deflation more readily than inflation. This is undoubtedly a fact of considerable impact on the distribution of adjustment costs in the real world. For instance, nations more averse to deflation than to inflation probably tend to accept a larger share of the transitional cost of adjustment when in surplus than when in deficit. Economic conflict is more likely to arise when such nations find themselves in deficit *vis-à-vis* nations with a greater aversion to inflation.[24] It is clear, therefore, that these differences must be taken into account.

(2) *Would the answer differ according to the country in which the initial disturbance causing the imbalance originates?* That is, would it differ according to whether the imbalance originates in an autonomous shift of demand or supply in the surplus country or in the

[23] The reader is cautioned to bear in mind that it is *solely* for the purposes of illustration and ease of exposition that "size" is chosen here as an example of a structural attribute. As we shall see in Chapter IV, the concept of the size of a nation is in actual fact insufficiently specific for formal analytical purposes.

[24] This is very much like the situation, described in Chapter II, now obtaining between the United States and the countries of continental Western Europe. Americans, apparently, are rather more averse to deflation than Europeans, whose greater concern by contrast is with the dangers of inflation. Conflict under such conditions is almost inevitable.

deficit country? This question is important because, also as suggested earlier, a country capable of transferring the transitional adjustment cost by initiating the adjustment process is likely to be a more serious source of instability in the international economic system than a nation lacking such a capability. Conversely, the extent to which the cost can actually be transferred by initiating the adjustment process is probably determined in part by the origin of the disturbance. Therefore, this difference too must be taken into account.

In considering these questions, suppose (still solely for purposes of illustration) we were to find that the very small nation, Littleland, should always be expected to pay the transitional cost of adjustment required by a payments imbalance, whether it is in deficit or surplus and whether the disturbance originates at home or abroad. We would have to conclude that a small nation, when considered *vis-à-vis* a much larger one, lacks completely the capacity to avoid transitional adjustment costs. To denote the extent to which the nation lacks this capacity, we may speak informally of its "adjustment vulnerability," referring simply to the proportion of the transitional cost which that nation must pay in the event of external imbalance. In this purely hypothetical example, the smaller country's adjustment vulnerability is infinite; the larger country's, zero.

Limitations and Implications of the Model

Many interesting conclusions concerning the international distribution of the transitional cost of adjustment can be extracted from an analysis of a two-country model such as that just described. Before proceeding to such an analysis, however, we should first take note of a serious limitation of the abstract two-country model that I am proposing to use—a limitation deriving from the fact that it is only in an abstract two-country model that two countries alone can appear to share the transitional adjustment cost entirely between themselves. In actual fact, in the real world of many countries, the distribution of that cost is rather more complex, primarily because of a tendency for it to reproduce itself—a tendency, in a real sense, to *multiply*.

To illustrate, suppose we add one country to our previous example, calling it for convenience Outland, and assume an initial condition of internal and external balance in all three nations. Now suppose that Bigland for some reason experiences a demand deflation and consequently reduces its foreign expenditures in its principal source of imports, Littleland; suppose too, that Bigland's adjustment vulnerability is near zero. Under these conditions, Littleland's adjustment vulnerability must be great, and it might react to its payments deficit, say, simply by deflating demand *pari passu* with Bigland until the deficit is eliminated. However, unless Littleland purchases all of its imports from Bigland, restoration of balance in Littleland's international payments is likely to mean some decline in exports from Outland. That is, Bigland's balance of payments will remain in partial surplus, and some of the transitional cost of adjustment will be shifted onto the third country. Not that Littleland's cost is thereby reduced; on the contrary, with fixed exchange rates, Littleland cannot avoid some demand deflation at home, given our assumption that Bigland's adjustment vulnerability is near zero. But, given the same assumption, now Outland must undergo some demand deflation, too. In effect, the transitional cost of adjustment has reproduced itself—multiplied. It could multiply further with the addition of yet more countries to our example.

Three countries are sufficient, however, to illustrate four important points. In the first place, our example highlights the "generality" of the adjustment process: the fact that some nations can approach payments balance by actually causing others to diverge from it. This appears to be impossible in an abstract two-country model where, owing to the restriction of the *ceteris paribus* assumption characteristic of partial-equilibrium analysis (in this case, the assumption that all other countries remain in payments balance), both countries can only move toward or away from balance simultaneously. But once the *ceteris paribus* assumption is relaxed—that is, once we begin to enter the more realistic world of general-equilibrium analysis—we see explicitly that imbalance and adjustment are in fact two sides of the same coin. One country will often adjust its own payments balance only by forcing another's payments into imbalance. And that country, too, will often achieve balance at the expense of yet another, and so on. Indeed, in the real world of many countries, very few members of the system can avoid being influenced by the process of payments adjustment, wherever the disturbance originates or whenever the adjustment begins. The entire system is one of interaction and interdependence.

The second point follows logically. That is, in the real world the international distribution of the transitional cost of adjustment is not a private matter to be settled by two nations experiencing bilateral imbalance. Quite the opposite. It is, in fact, a matter of considerable power play, where the capacity of each country to avoid transitional adjustment costs is matched against that of every other country, where the less vulnerable countries continually transfer these costs onto the more vulnerable, and consequently where the most vulnerable countries pay the largest total adjustment cost of all.

Third, it is evident that in practice this interplay of national power is expressed in the kinds of adjustment techniques employed by all of the affected countries. In our simple example, the kind of technique (demand deflation) employed to eliminate Littleland's deficit was distinctly negative, owing to the crucial assumption that Bigland's adjustment vulnerability was near zero. Consequently, the transitional cost of adjustment was correspondingly large, and it was paid entirely by Littleland. Had that assumption not been made, however, alternative approaches to the adjustment process of a more positive kind would have been feasible. For instance, Littleland might have been able to innovate to improve its technology or the quality of its products, or it might have promoted foreign sales to substitute for those previously lost in Bigland. Consequently, the cost of adjustment would have been rather smaller; and, significantly, some of it would have been paid by Bigland. Indeed, all of the cost would have been paid by Bigland, had that country simply reacted to its own initial demand deflation by reflating internal money incomes and prices.

Thus we see again how the choice of adjustment techniques determines both the magnitude and the international distribution of transitional costs of adjustment. More importantly, we see now how the choice of those techniques expresses the adjustment vulnerability of each of the countries concerned—that is, how it expresses their capacity, relative to one another, for avoiding the transitional cost of adjustment. If the surplus country has the greater capacity, the techniques employed by it and by the deficit country to eliminate their mutual imbalance are apt to be negative, with transitional adjustment costs falling heavily on the deficit country regardless of where the disturbance originates. Only if the latter of the two countries has the greater capacity is it likely that their approach to the adjustment process will be positive, with transitional costs falling more heavily or entirely on the surplus country.

This implies our last point: that there is a sharp divergence between national and cosmopolitan viewpoints concerning the most equitable distribution of the transitional adjustment cost. Recall that we are discussing in this study only situations of payments imbalance where real adjustment is required.[25] Such an imbalance may be caused by monetary phenomena—expansion in one country or contraction in another—or it may be caused by developments of a more "structural" nature, including most importantly changes in consumer demand, technology, or the supply of labor and capital. Using a cosmopolitan criterion of equity, we may argue that in the event of imbalances caused by *monetary* phenomena the transitional cost of adjustment is most equitably distributed when it is always paid wholly

[25] That is, we are not discussing imbalances of payments caused by temporary and nonrepetitive events, like an earthquake or a crop failure, for which financing rather than real adjustment is the appropriate response. See above, Chapter II, fn. 9.

by the country in which the disturbance originates.[26] In other words, if one country (like Bigland) undergoes demand deflation causing deficits elsewhere, it ought to be that country's responsibility to eliminate the imbalance by monetary expansion or other positive techniques. Other nations should not be compelled to contract demand because of internal monetary developments in the first. Conversely, if one country inflates excessively, it should be that country—not others —that is compelled to pay the adjustment cost. To state the rule more formally: for imbalances caused by monetary phenomena, the distribution of the transitional cost of adjustment is "best," from a cosmopolitan point of view, when each nation's adjustment vulnerability is infinite for disturbances originating at home and zero for disturbances originating abroad.

In cases of imbalances caused by *structural* developments, on the other hand, a set rule is more difficult to formulate. Suppose a country suddenly experiences a payments deficit because of a shift of consumer tastes away from home goods in favor of imports. Should that country be expected to pay *all* of the adjustment cost, contracting demand until such time as the deficit is wholly eliminated? Should other nations be expected to pay *none*, refraining entirely from monetary expansion despite the net increase of demand for their products? Presumably, in a case such as this, all nations would be expected to share the cost together, though in what proportions it is impossible to say *a priori*. Similarly, all countries ought to share the adjustment cost required by other kinds of structural changes involving technology or factor endowments, though again the proportions are uncertain. Perhaps all we can say with certainty is that for imbalances caused by structural developments, the distribution of the transitional cost of adjustment is "best," from a cosmopolitan point of view, when each nation's adjustment vulnerability is less than infinity but greater than zero.

From the national point of view, however, the "best" distribution is radically different, whatever the cause of the disturbance or its origin. For any one country, the smaller the transitional adjustment cost, the better; and the best is zero. Ideally, each country individually would prefer to be totally invulnerable to external pressures. Few nations have ever achieved such invulnerability, though I might suggest that the United States achieved what was certainly a close approximation during the first postwar decade. This was the period of the dollar shortage, when the rest of the world had little choice but to adapt to the state of the American balance of payments, and when the per-

[26] Once again, I am ignoring the empirical difficulties—which admittedly may be very serious—of identifying the source of specific balance-of-payments disturbances in the real world.

formance of the American economy was indifferent to disturbances originating abroad. This was the period when—to recall Dennis Robertson's famous aphorism—if the United States sneezed, Europe caught a cold. True, the approximation was not perfect: the United States, feeling compelled to share at least part of the transitional adjustment cost, undertook, for this reason among others, to build up foreign dollar balances by offering foreign aid and by encouraging American private investments abroad. But this only indicates how difficult it is for *any* country to reduce its adjustment vulnerability all the way to zero.

Even so, each country individually has an incentive to reduce its adjustment vulnerability to a minimum. Therefore, each country will, instinctively but also quite logically, seek continually to modify its own structural attributes so as to minimize its future adjustment costs. This should help to explain a variety of observable phenomena, such as the seemingly "irrational" ways in which nations formulate commercial policies and negotiate to modify them.

What are the principal structural attributes of nations that can be said to determine the international distribution of transitional costs of balance-of-payments adjustment?

One attribute that springs immediately to mind is "size." Certainly it seems appropriate, at first glance, to differentiate analytically large nations from small nations, and to compare the capacity of the two to avoid the transitional cost of adjustment required by external imbalance. But, in fact, this would not be an appropriate procedure. For size is an ambiguous notion, too lacking in precise content and too difficult to measure to be of much use in any formal economic analysis. Even at an international conference of distinguished economists gathered some years ago to discuss the "economic consequences of the size of nations," agreement on one single measure proved impossible.[27] Some participants in the conference proposed population as the proper index of the size of nations; others, the level of real national income per capita; still others, market volume or geographic area. No one index proved satisfactory; the most the conferees could agree to was that "one has to be prepared to discuss not one single concept of size, but any or all of several concepts."[28]

But if in effect one must treat separately each of the structural factors that together define the size of nations, then why make use of the intermediate term at all? The answer has to do with both convenience and convention. Nations are typically classified as large or small, mainly because the terms happen to be a handy catch-all device for describing one or another combination of quite specific structural attributes. In certain limited contexts, where the combination is clearly labelled or understood, such a practice may be considered perfectly legitimate, and I shall revert to it briefly when summarizing our discussion in the last chapter of this study. Likewise, I shall revert in the last chapter to referring to a country's "level of economic development," though this, too, is an intermediate notion.[29] For now, however, I propose to concentrate on a small number of specific structural attributes whose content—and influence on the distribution of transitional adjustment costs—is more precise.

[27] See E. A. G. Robinson (ed.), *Economic Consequences of the Size of Nations*, Proceedings of a Conference held by the International Economic Association (London: Macmillan, 1960); especially, Robinson, "Introduction," p. xv.

[28] *Ibid.*

[29] See, for example, P. T. Bauer and B. S. Yamey, *The Economics of Under-Developed Countries* (Cambridge: Cambridge University Press, 1957), pp. 3-7.

In my opinion, four structural attributes are particularly important in determining the international distribution of transitional costs of adjustment. These are (1) diversification of production, (2) degree of industrialization, (3) international investment status, and (4) secular growth rate. This list could possibly be extended to include other attributes, but their significance, I believe, would prove to be marginal at best.

Diversification in Production

Nations can be unambiguously differentiated according to their diversification in production. It is an empirical fact that some countries are more specialized economically than others. That is, in some countries the production structure—the proportional distribution of output and resources—shows a high degree of concentration in relatively few industries (including agriculture and mining), whereas in others a much fuller variety of industries can be observed. As it happens, the latter, the diversified economies, are mostly located in the developed Northern and Western portions of the globe. Conversely, it is in the less developed South and East primarily that we find the specialized economies—that is, the economies in which many of the full variety of industries observed elsewhere are either lacking or barely represented. But there also happens to be practically as much variation in the degree of productive specialization within each of these two broad areas of the world as there is between them. Diversification in production, therefore, is a useful basis for differentiating countries not only between the two areas but within each of them as well.

Since this is the case, we can proceed to ask the following question: what would be the distribution of transitional adjustment costs between two countries roughly comparable in all features except the diversification of their production structures? Would a relatively specialized nation be compelled to pay all of the transitional cost of adjustment when considered *vis-à-vis* a more diversified nation, or none of it?

To begin with, we may note the obvious: that specialized nations are likely to be more highly dependent upon foreign markets with respect to both exports and imports than diversified nations. That is, specialized economies are likely to be more "open."[30] This follows not only from the greater concentration of their production structures, but also from the precepts of the pure theory of international trade. Foreign trade provides an effective "escape" from the disadvantages of

[30] See Simon Kuznets, "Economic Growth of Small Nations," pp. 18-23; and G. Marcy, "How Far Can Foreign Trade and Customs Agreements Confer Upon Small Nations the Advantages of Large Nations?", pp. 266-268, in Robinson (editor), *op. cit.*

specialization. Although many countries are unable to produce efficiently a wide variety of goods and services, they can nevertheless achieve comparatively high living standards by specializing in the lines of production for which they are best fitted by natural advantages. In other words, goods and services not produced at home can be purchased abroad, and imports can be paid for with exports. Dependence on foreign trade, then, is the Siamese twin of productive specialization. And the greater the degree of specialization, the greater the dependence on foreign trade—the "openness"—as measured by the proportion of foreign trade to national income.[31] The extreme is reached in the familiar one-or-two-crop country, the monetized portion of whose economy is overwhelmingly concentrated in production for export.

However, while trade provides an escape from the disadvantages of specialization, it is a somewhat precarious escape.[32] For openness exposes the specialized nation—whether it is industrialized or a primary producer[33]—to all kinds of external pressures, and greatly increases its adjustment vulnerability. Indeed, it implies that a specialized nation must pay a disproportionately large share of the transitional cost of balance-of-payments adjustment when considered *vis-à-vis* a diversified nation. This may be deduced by comparing several aspects of the specialized nation's dependence on foreign trade with the relative nondependence of the more diversified nation (assuming still that the two countries are roughly comparable in all other features).

In the first place, the production of a specialized nation tends more than that of a diversified nation to be confined to a narrow range of output not only for home consumption but also—and even more importantly—for export. Frequently, as few as one, two, or three products account for as much as half the country's national income, and for two-thirds to virtually all of its exports. This renders the specialized nation particularly vulnerable to disruptions of its foreign markets, since a given absolute change in exports of a single commodity means a comparatively greater change in the balance of payments of a specialized nation, relative to the total volume of domestic output, than

---

[31] It should be noted that a high proportion of foreign trade to national income does not necessarily mean a high absolute volume of foreign trade. Indeed, the case is usually the reverse; it is typically the diversified economies, relatively not dependent on trade, that have the largest absolute trade volume.

[32] See Kuznets, *loc. cit.*; L. Tarshis, "The Size of the Economy and Its relation to Stability and Steady Progress," pp. 190-199; R. Triffin, "The Size of the Nation and its Vulnerability to Economic Nationalism," pp. 247-264; and Marcy, *loc. cit.*, in Robinson (ed.), *op. cit.*

[33] Kindleberger writes, concerning the "risks" of specialization, that "advanced countries are as vulnerable as the underdeveloped." Charles P. Kindleberger, *Foreign Trade and the National Economy* (New Haven: Yale University Press, 1962), p. 224.

in the balance of payments of a more diversified nation. This is true, of course, whether the disruption takes the form of an autonomous increase of foreign demand or a decrease. And, since with a high degree of specialization there is only a small chance of offsetting movements, this means that the specialized country normally has little choice but to react immediately to disturbances originating abroad, bearing via inflation or deflation of aggregate demand the greater share of the transitional cost of adjustment.[34]

This tendency is aggravated by the fact that, in addition, the export sales of specialized nations tend to be confined ordinarily to a rather narrow range of national markets abroad. That is, a specialized nation commonly relies on just a few trading partners—frequently no more than two or three—for the great bulk of its foreign receipts. This is in contrast to a more diversified nation which, owing to the greater variety of its trade, can more easily direct exports into a larger number of channels. And it suggests a further degree of vulnerability for the specialized country, since disruption of just one foreign market (say, the more diversified country) implies a comparatively greater imbalance relative to domestic output.

To be sure, much of this vulnerability to disturbances originating abroad could be eliminated if, in fact, a specialized nation were the dominant world supplier of its principal export commodity, and could somehow (through a private export cartel, perhaps, or a state trading organization) use its quasi-monopoly power over the price and quantity of its exports to stabilize its foreign-exchange earnings. In practice, however, specialized nations find it virtually impossible to exercise anything like monopoly power in world markets, either because cooperation with other exporting countries is too difficult, or because of the presence of competing products in importing countries. Consequently, the specialized country typically pays a disproportionate

[34] In this connection, see Benton F. Massell, "Export Concentration and Fluctuations in Export Earnings: A Cross-Section Analysis," *American Economic Review*, Vol. LIV (March 1964), pp. 47-63. Using regression techniques, Massell could find very little evidence of a relationship between instability of export earnings and concentration of exports. However, this is not inconsistent with the argument in the text that the more specialized nation has the higher adjustment vulnerability because its exports are more concentrated in a narrow range of products. For, what matters, as Massell himself acknowledges, is the fact that "a given degree of export instability has a greater impact on the economy" the greater the dependence on foreign trade (p. 62). Moreover, Massell's own statistics indicate that the specialized nations do tend to experience the *greatest* degree of export instability; and these statistics are confirmed in a study recently completed by the research staff of the IBRD. See Dragoslav Avramovic and associates, *Economic Growth and External Debt* (Baltimore: Johns Hopkins Press, 1964), pp. 14-19.

share of the transitional cost of adjustment in the event of payments disturbances originating in more diversified countries.[35]

The specialized country also tends to pay a disproportionate share of the transitional cost of adjustment in the event of payments disturbances originating at home—that is, in the event of imbalances *vis-à-vis* the more diversified country arising from autonomous increases or decreases of demand or supply in the specialized country. Consider the case of domestic demand inflation. Demand inflation in a specialized country will tend immediately to generate an increase in the volume of its imports, since its specialization implies a comparatively high marginal propensity to import. But since a specialized country is obliged to import a wide variety of products, and since in any event its absolute volume of trade is not likely to be sizable, it can exercise via, say, a state trading organization, very little monopsonistic power in any world market. Therefore, the pressure to adjust exerted on the more diversified country will be rather slight in relation to its own domestic output. The pressure on the specialized country, on the other hand, will be considerably greater. And this would be as true in a case of demand deflation there as in one of inflation.

A specialized country is therefore in an unenviable position *vis-à-vis* a diversified one. Because of its openness, it must in effect make itself an economic satellite of its more diversified neighbor. Since a specialized country lacks the power to influence world markets, and since autarky is extremely expensive, it has no choice but to adapt its national production structure continually in response to external or, for that matter, internal pressures. "It must ride the waves of economic change if it is not to be overwhelmed."[36] In brief, the adjustment vulnerability of a specialized country *vis-à-vis* a more diversified country is virtually infinite, and this is true whether the specialized country is in deficit or in surplus, and whether the disturbance originates at home or abroad.

[35] In other words, a more diversified country has the capacity to avoid the cost of adjustment by transferring it to others. Furthermore, it tends to make use of its capacity. Kravis writes of "the inherent tendency of any large area composed of diverse interests to reconcile conflicts over the resolution of domestic difficulties by shifting as much of the burden of adjustment to outsiders as possible. This is evident in U.S. commercial policy." Irving B. Kravis, "The U. S. Trade Position and the Common Market," *Factors Affecting the United States Balance of Payments*, Papers Submitted to the Joint Economic Committee of the Congress (Washington, D.C.: 1962), p. 100.

[36] Carl Major Wright, *Economic Adaptation to a Changing World Market* (Copenhagen: Ejnar Munksgaard, 1939), p. 245. See also Kuznets, *loc. cit.*; and Triffin, *loc. cit.*

Degree of Industrialization

Quite apart from their general degree of diversification in all kinds of production, nations can also be differentiated according to their relative specialization in certain kinds of production—most broadly, in either industrial or primary production. That is, several economies, each having a range of industries of roughly the same dimensions, may nevertheless be quite different in orientation, some being predominantly industrial, others being mainly agricultural or mining. By and large, it seems true that the latter group, the producers of primary commodities, have by far the greater adjustment vulnerability. The principal evidence for this argument is the simple fact that the export receipts of primary producing countries are notoriously unstable, reflecting large and frequent changes of both quantities and prices.

This matter of export instability is a much more serious problem for primary producers than for industrial countries, the prices of whose exports are determined primarily on a cost basis and therefore tend to change only moderately in the short run. Primary producers, by contrast, have no choice but to export at prices that, in the short run at least, are determined independently of them in world commodity markets (their factor returns adjusting accordingly). Consequently, they have no choice but to adapt, as often as is necessary, by inflating or deflating, as prices in these markets rise or fall. It is they, in other words, not industrial nations, who are compelled to accommodate to emerging payments imbalances, just as it was this class of countries that did the accommodating in the nineteenth century when Britain was the world's largest importer of primary commodities. Furthermore, it really makes little difference for the primary producing countries whether the frequent fluctuations of commodity prices originate in variations of supply conditions or in variations of demand (reflecting the business cycle of industrial countries). Whatever the source of disturbances, the primary producers seem to pay the bulk of transitional adjustment costs.

It follows from what has just been said that the adjustment vulnerability of a country will be greater, the greater the degree of its productive specialization in agriculture and mining. It is easy to understand, therefore, why the primary producing countries in the world today are so insistent in their demand for commodity stabilization agreements and compensatory finance. It is also easy to understand their seemingly "irrational" preference for industrial production. These are actually fundamentally rational responses to a disproportionately high-cost situation.

International Investment Status

Some countries regularly export capital on a large scale; others are capital importers. This is yet another basis for differentiating between countries. And it is an important system of differentiation because it bears directly upon our subject. Capital-exporting nations typically can react to a payments disturbance with a variation of interest rates, slowing down or speeding up the rate of capital outflow and thereby maintaining external balance. (This was the method used by the United Kingdom in the nineteenth century to avoid transitional adjustment costs.) This tends to force capital-importing nations to make the necessary accommodation to balance-of-payments disturbances, wherever they originate, since for them control of the rate of capital flow is much more difficult. Capital importers, in other words, have a relatively high adjustment vulnerability.

Related to this is the special vulnerability all nations feel *vis-à-vis* reserve-currency countries. One of the major complaints of the nations of Western Europe in their present confrontation with the United States is that America is not paying its share of the transitional cost of adjustment. Under the gold-exchange standard, they argue, the reserve-currency country has the unique advantage of being largely freed from balance-of-payments constraints: it can expect others to "lend" to it—that is, accept balances of its currency—to the amount of any deficit it happens to incur; and it can expect the deficit to continue until the others make the necessary accommodation. There is a good deal of truth in this proposition, though probably not so much as the Europeans themselves believe. At any rate, it indicates that non-reserve-currency countries must pay a disproportionate share of the transitional cost of adjustment *vis-à-vis* reserve-currency countries (at least when the latter are in deficit).

Secular Growth Rate

For reasons that are not altogether clear but that seem related to their economic structures, some countries tend to enjoy over an extended period a very high rate of economic growth. Over the same period other countries may experience only moderate growth or even stagnation or decline. Here is one more important basis for differentiating between countries: their secular growth rates, both absolute and relative. In fact, this is a system of classification frequently employed by economists. Linder, for instance speaks of "acting" and "reacting" countries:

> We categorize countries as acting or reacting. An acting country is growing faster than other countries. It may be moving ahead of

the main group of countries or it might be catching up with this group. A reacting country is growing less rapidly than other countries or in the process of having its lead lessened. . . . The reason why a relatively stagnant country is [categorized as] reacting is because the movement of the acting country is making it necessary for it continually to adapt to changing circumstances. These are the "hazards of trade."[37]

When Linder refers to the "hazards of trade," he is in fact describing the notion of adjustment vulnerability. Reacting countries grow less rapidly than others over the long term. Consequently, their capacity to avoid transitional adjustment costs is weakened, and in the short term they must adapt—accommodate—to balance-of-payments disturbances arising out of the action of more rapidly growing nations. Presumably they must also correct for their own disturbances. They are, in other words, disproportionately vulnerable to external pressures.[38]

[37] Staffan B. Linder, *An Essay on Trade and Transformation* (New York: Wiley and Company, 1961), pp. 143-144.
[38] See K. M. Savosnick, "Economic Growth and Balance of Payments Problems," in Roy Harrod and D. C. Hague (eds.), *International Trade Theory in a Developing World*, Proceedings of a Conference held by the International Economic Association (London: Macmillan, 1963), pp. 297-308.

I have mentioned four structural attributes of nations that are especially significant in determining the international distribution of transitional costs of balance-of-payments adjustment. The world economy does not lack specific examples of countries featuring one or another combination of these attributes—countries whose adjustment vulnerability, consequently, tends to be very great.

For example, the weaknesses of the economy of Ceylon were recently discussed in precisely these terms in the columns of *The Economist*: "The trouble with this particular economy is its vulnerability. When America sneezes Europe only catches cold; poor Ceylon tends to get the flu."[39] The journal lays heavy emphasis on Ceylon's marked specialization in production, particularly in primary production. Three commodities alone—tea, rubber, and coconut products—account for one-fourth of Ceylon's national income and for nine-tenths of its exports. In none of the three, however, does the country exercise anything approaching monopoly power in world markets. This makes Ceylon's economy extremely open, exposing it to all kinds of external pressures. When, for instance, devastating hurricanes in the Caribbean in 1964 boosted the world price of sugar—a vital Ceylonese import—Ceylon was compelled to accommodate fully to the disturbance by cutting back other imports and slowing down its development programs. Furthermore, Ceylon must accommodate fully to disturbances originating at home as well. No other country paid any of the transitional cost of adjustment in 1965, for instance, when the Ceylonese rice crop failed.

Oskar Morgenstern suggests another example: Hungary in the interwar period.[40] At that time the Hungarian economy was overwhelmingly specialized in the production of an agricultural commodity, wheat, yet the country lacked any world monopolistic power since its exports were totally insignificant in the international wheat market. Consequently, when during the Great Depression foreign demand shrank, Hungary was compelled to accommodate fully by undergoing a catastrophic deflation. Morgenstern contrasts the vulnerability of this open economy with the relative invulnerability during the same period of another wheat exporter, Canada. He attributes the difference mainly to the greater diversification of the Canadian production structure.[41]

[39] "Tea and Tamil," *The Economist*, Volume CCXV (April 3, 1965), p. 33.

[40] Oskar Morgenstern, "Die Macht im Handel der Staaten: Ein Problem der Theorie des internationalen Handels," *Jahrbuch für Sozialwissenschaft* (1963), p. 50.

[41] *Ibid.* He also attributes this difference partly to a technical innovation through which hard Canadian wheat came to be preferred to the soft wheat that Hungary produced.

Additional examples readily suggest themselves. As a matter of fact, the world economy today is literally dotted with small countries, heavily dependent on primary production and on capital imports, whose overspecialized and often stagnant economies are especially vulnerable to external pressures. These are the less developed countries of Asia, Africa, and Latin America, manifestly the weakest members of the international economic system, and consequently the nations with the highest adjustment vulnerability. Indeed, in situations of payments imbalance *vis-à-vis* the industrial and capital-exporting countries, the adjustment vulnerability of the less developed countries approaches infinity. Wherever disturbances originate and for whatever cause, it is these countries that must ordinarily make the necessary accommodation; and ordinarily the accommodation that they must make is negative rather than positive, since (owing to their intense desire to import finished consumer and capital goods) they are much more often in payments deficit than in surplus. In short, the less developed countries as a group suffer from an inequitable distribution of transitional adjustment costs. They must pay a disproportionately large share of these costs and, in addition, the costs that they must pay are disproportionately high.

Furthermore, the international economy is almost always in transition, with new disturbances always emerging to keep the system in a state of more or less constant flux. For countries with high adjustment vulnerability, such a situation is intolerably costly. No wonder, then, that so many of the less developed countries show a strong preference for industrial production and seek to devise commercial and financial policies designed to stimulate diversification, even into inefficient lines of production.

The conventional theory of international trade assures us that such behavior is "irrational"; production not based on comparative advantage reduces a nation's real national income. But so, too, does specialization based wholly on comparative advantage that results in a continual and costly reallocation of resources at the margin. In actual fact, by diversifying its production structure, and in particular by initiating industrialization, a country may be able to *increase* its real income, to the extent that the income saved as a result of the reduction of its adjustment vulnerability exceeds the income lost as a result of the deviation from its comparative advantage. By any economic standard such behavior must be judged entirely rational.

The point can be illustrated by means of a very simple diagram. In Figure 1, the horizontal axis measures the degree of diversification of a country's production structure: at the origin the country is specialized completely in the production of just one commodity (sugar, cocoa, tin, copper, bananas, etc.), at points further along to the right

FIGURE 1

MARGINAL NATIONAL-INCOME CHANGES ASSOCIATED WITH CHANGES IN THE
DEGREE OF DIVERSIFICATION OF A COUNTRY'S PRODUCTION STRUCTURE.

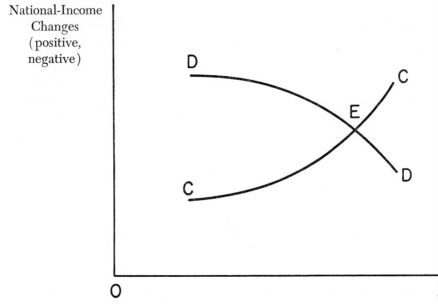

Degree of Diversification

the country's economic structure includes increasingly inefficient lines
of production, and at Z the country is autarkic. The vertical axis
measures changes in the country's real national income. The gains of
national income resulting from the diversification of the country's production structure are measured along the curve labelled DD. The
losses of national income resulting from the simultaneous deviation
from the country's comparative advantage are measured along the
curve labelled CC. At point E the income saved as a result of a further
reduction of the country's adjustment vulnerability just equals the income lost as a result of a further deviation from its comparative advantage. Just how many less developed countries are located in the
range to the left of E, where marginal gains exceed marginal losses, is
a moot point—what is certain is that most less developed countries view
themselves as being located there. Hence, it is not surprising that so
many of them insist on policies of diversification and industrialization.

Such policies require vast amounts of long-term development capital, particularly in the form of capital imports. This capital is, unfortunately, all too difficult to accumulate in a setting where the volume of domestic saving is limited by the low level of per-capita incomes, where export earnings are limited by protectionist policies and inelastic demand in the developed world, where potential foreign investors prefer to confine their ventures mainly to the industrial and financial centers, and where the donors of foreign aid are in practice becoming increasingly niggardly. In such a setting, less developed countries are obliged to draw upon whatever resources they can obtain, including their own international monetary reserves. To be sure, this is not the normal function of reserves, which are presumably held as a safeguard against future contingencies rather than to finance current purchases. And certainly the developing nations are conscious of the advantages of having adequate reserves. But such is the sense of urgency in these nations that even their exchange reserves are used for capital imports. Once their reserves are exhausted, however, these vulnerable nations are even less capable than before of defending themselves against external pressures—at least against payments deficits, the variety of external pressure to which the less developed countries are most prone. As a result, they find that the share of transitional adjustment costs they must pay is as large as ever.

What we see here is another in the series of vicious circles enmeshing the less developed countries. Because they are overspecialized and concentrate in primary production, developing nations have a relatively high adjustment vulnerability. To reduce their vulnerability they seek to diversify and industrialize. Because of the inadequate supply of development resources available to them, they fall back on their exchange reserves to finance many of their capital imports. But, with their reserves diminished, they find themselves no less vulnerable to external pressures than before.

How can this vicious circle be broken? The solution, clearly, lies in a sizable increase in the amount of economic assistance being provided to the developing nations. Additional assistance could, of course, be provided through many channels, most of which are already under discussion. The industrial nations often speak affirmatively, if vaguely, of reforming trade policies, of providing new incentives and guarantees for private foreign investments in less developed countries, and of augmenting bilateral and multilateral aid programs. Strangely, though, little is said, affirmatively at least, about what could prove to be one of the most important channels of all—world monetary reform.

A good deal of assistance could be provided to the developing nations by distributing to them the largest part of any new reserves that are created as a consequence of world monetary reform. For the creation of new reserves effects a saving of real resources, and these resources might just as conveniently accrue to the less developed countries as to any others. As Fritz Machlup has so rightly emphasized:

> The discovery that international money can be produced with cheap ink and paper, and need not be produced with hard work applied to metal dug out of the ground, affords a large saving. . . . The savings in the production of the low-cost substitute must be distributed somehow . . . the saving will benefit someone and its distribution must needs be arbitrary.[42]

Unfortunately, the leading nations object to any such prospective linking of the problems of international liquidity and economic development. According to the Group of Ten, "the provision of capital to developing countries is a problem quite distinct from the creation of reserves and should be achieved by other techniques."[43] Underlying this objection is the view that the less developed countries should not be granted "something for nothing." As a matter of fact, the opposite is the case: the two problems are already closely linked by the fact that the less developed countries at present must actually *pay* a very considerable "something for nothing" because of the strikingly inequitable distribution of transitional adjustment costs. Nations seek, whenever possible and irrespective of the origin or cause of disturbances, to transfer their transitional adjustment costs onto their weaker trading partners. It is a fact that, in the international economic system, the less developed countries are the weakest trading partners of all. Hence, these countries must pay the largest total adjustment cost, without even the benefit of a *quid pro quo*. It seems only reasonable, therefore, since monetary reform does involve a saving whose distribution is in any event a matter of deliberate choice, to let the main benefit accrue to those who until now have been obliged to pay the highest price for the privilege of membership in the system. And it seems only equitable to let the benefit accrue roughly in proportion to the present distribution of adjustment costs.

Technically, the problems of liquidity and development can be linked rather easily. Certainly, it would not be difficult for the reserve agency—whether it be an expanded International Monetary Fund or some other institution—to get any newly created reserves, whatever

---

[42] Fritz Machlup, "The Cloakroom Rule of International Reserves: Reserve Creation and Resources Transfer," *Quarterly Journal of Economics*, Vol. LXXIX (August 1965), pp. 353-355.

[43] Group of Ten, *Report of the Study Group on the Creation of Reserve Assets*, *Report to the Deputies of the Group of Ten*, May 31, 1965, pp. 69-70. Also, see *Guidelines for Improving the International Monetary System*, Report of the Subcommittee on International Exchange and Payments of the Joint Economic Committee of the Congress (Washington, D.C.: 1965), pp. 11-12.

their form and amount, into the hands of the less developed countries. For instance, it could invest in fresh debt obligations issued by the World Bank or its affiliates, or it could even buy government securities issued directly by the less developed countries themselves.[44] Nor would it be particularly difficult for the agency to ensure that the newly created reserves are properly employed by their recipients to help reduce their rather marked adjustment vulnerability. On practical grounds, therefore, there seem to be no really critical objections to this pattern of distribution.

This is not to suggest that an approach to the problem of economic development via world monetary reform is preferable to all other types of aid schemes. It has been my intention only to demonstrate that there is a logical connection between these two areas of concern. In fact, all approaches to the development problem are useful; all are preferable to the vicious circle of adjustment vulnerability and reserve exhaustion that presently entraps the less developed countries of the world.

[44] See United Nations Trade and Development Board, *International Monetary Issues and the Developing Countries, Report of the Group of Experts,* November 1, 1965. See also "To the Aid of Aid," *The Economist,* Vol. CCXVII (October 9, 1965), pp. 193-194, for an interesting proposal for linking the problems of international liquidity and economic development without providing new reserves directly to the less developed countries.

PUBLICATIONS OF THE
INTERNATIONAL FINANCE SECTION

The International Finance Section publishes at irregular intervals papers in four series: ESSAYS IN INTERNATIONAL FINANCE, PRINCETON STUDIES IN INTERNATIONAL FINANCE, SPECIAL PAPERS IN INTERNATIONAL ECONOMICS and REPRINTS IN INTERNATIONAL FINANCE. All four of these may be ordered directly from the Section.

Single copies of the ESSAYS and REPRINTS are distributed without charge to all interested persons, both here and abroad. Additional copies of any one issue may be obtained from the Section at a charge of $0.25 a copy, payable in advance. This charge may be waived to foreign institutions of education or research.

For the STUDIES and SPECIAL PAPERS there will be a charge of $1.00 a copy. This charge will be waived on copies distributed to college and university libraries here and abroad. In addition, the charge is sometimes waived on single copies requested by persons residing abroad who find it difficult to make remittance.

For the convenience of our British customers, arrangements have been made for retail distribution of the STUDIES and SPECIAL PAPERS through the Economists' Bookshop, Portugal Street, London, W.C. 2, and Blackwells, Broad Street, Oxford. These booksellers will usually have our publications in stock.

A mailing list is maintained for the distribution of ESSAYS and RE-PRINTS as they are issued and of announcements of new issues in the series of STUDIES and SPECIAL PAPERS. Requests for inclusion in this list will be honored, except that students will not be placed on the permanent mailing list, because waste results from frequent changes of addresses.

The following is a complete list of the publications of the International Finance Section. The issues of the four series that are still available from the Section are marked by asterisks. Those marked by daggers are out of stock at the International Finance Section but may be obtained in xerographic reproductions (that is, looking like the originals) from University Microfilms, Inc., 313 N. First Street, Ann Arbor, Michigan 48107. (Most of the issues are priced at $3.00.)

ESSAYS IN INTERNATIONAL FINANCE

†No. 1. Friedrich A. Lutz, International Monetary Mechanisms: The Keynes and White Proposals. (July 1943)

† 2. Frank D. Graham, Fundamentals of International Monetary Policy. (Autumn 1943)

† 3. Richard A. Lester, International Aspects of Wartime Monetary Experience. (Aug. 1944)

† 4. Ragnar Nurkse, Conditions of International Monetary Equilibrium. (Spring 1945)

† 5. Howard S. Ellis, Bilateralism and the Future of International Trade. (Summer 1945)

† 6. Arthur I. Bloomfield, The British Balance-of-Payments Problem. (Autumn 1945)

† 7. Frank A. Southard, Jr., Some European Currency and Exchange Experiences. (Summer 1946)

† 8. Miroslav A. Kriz, Postwar International Lending. (Spring 1947)

† 9. Friedrich A. Lutz, The Marshall Plan and European Economic Policy. (Spring 1948)

† 10. Frank D. Graham, The Cause and Cure of "Dollar Shortage." (Jan. 1949)

† 11. Horst Mendershausen, Dollar Shortage and Oil Surplus in 1949-1950. (Nov. 1950)

† 12. Sir Arthur Salter, Foreign Investment. (Feb. 1951)

† 13. Sir Roy Harrod, The Pound Sterling. (Feb. 1952)

† 14. S. Herbert Frankel, Some Conceptual Aspects of International Economic Development of Underdeveloped Territories. (May 1952)

† 15. Miroslav A. Kriz, The Price of Gold. (July 1952)

† 16. William Diebold, Jr., The End of the I.T.O. (Oct. 1952)

† 17. Sir Douglas Copland, Problems of the Sterling Area: With Special Reference to Australia. (Sept. 1953)

† 18. Raymond F. Mikesell, The Emerging Pattern of International Payments. (April 1954)

† 19. D. Gale Johnson, Agricultural Price Policy and International Trade. (June 1954)

† 20. Ida Greaves, "The Colonial Sterling Balances." (Sept. 1954)

† 21. Raymond Vernon, America's Foreign Trade Policy and the GATT. (Oct. 1954)

† 22. Roger Auboin, The Bank for International Settlements, 1930-1955. (May 1955)

† 23. Wytze Gorter, United States Merchant Marine Policies: Some International Implications. (June 1955)

† 24. Thomas C. Schelling, International Cost-Sharing Arrangements. (Sept. 1955)

† 25. James E. Meade, The Belgium-Luxembourg Economic Union, 1921-1939. (March 1956)

† 26. Samuel I. Katz, Two Approaches to the Exchange-Rate Problem: The United Kingdom and Canada. (Aug. 1956)

† 27. A. R. Conan, The Changing Pattern of International Investment in Selected Sterling Countries. (Dec. 1956)

† 28. Fred H. Klopstock, The International Status of the Dollar. (May 1957)

† 29. Raymond Vernon, Trade Policy in Crisis. (March 1958)

† 30. Sir Roy Harrod, The Pound Sterling, 1951-1958. (Aug. 1958)

† 31. Randall Hinshaw, Toward European Convertibility. (Nov. 1958)

† 32. Francis H. Schott, The Evolution of Latin American Exchange-Rate Policies since World War II. (Jan. 1959)

† 33. Alec Cairncross. The International Bank for Reconstruction and Development. (March 1959)

† 34. Miroslav A. Kriz, Gold in World Monetary Affairs Today. (June 1959)

37

† 35. Sir Donald MacDougall, The Dollar Problem: A Reappraisal. (Nov. 1960)
† 36. Brian Tew, The International Monetary Fund: Its Present Role and Future Prospect. (March 1961)
† 37. Samuel I. Katz, Sterling Speculation and European Convertibility: 1955-1958. (Oct. 1961)
† 38. Boris C. Swerling, Current Issues in International Commodity Policy. (June 1962)
† 39. Pieter Lieftinck, Recent Trends in International Monetary Policies. (Sept. 1962)
† 40. Jerome L. Stein, The Nature and Efficiency of the Foreign Exchange Market. (Oct. 1962)
† 41. Friedrich A. Lutz, The Problem of International Liquidity and the Multiple-Currency Standard. (March 1963)
† 42. Sir Dennis Robertson, A Memorandum Submitted to the Canadian Royal Commission on Banking and Finance. (May 1963)
† 43. Marius W. Holtrop, Monetary Policy in an Open Economy: Its Objectives, Instruments, Limitations, and Dilemmas. (Sept. 1963)
† 44. Harry G. Johnson, Alternative Guiding Principles for the Use of Monetary Policy. (Nov. 1963)
† 45. Jacob Viner, Problems of Monetary Control. (May 1964)
† 46. Charles P. Kindleberger, Balance-of-Payments Deficits and the International Market for Liquidity. (May 1965)
† 47. Jacques Rueff and Fred Hirsch, The Role and the Rule of Gold: An Argument. (June 1965)
† 48. Sidney Weintraub, The Foreign-Exchange Gap of the Developing Countries. (Sept. 1965)
† 49. Tibor Scitovsky, Requirements of an International Reserve System. (Oct. 1965)
* 50. John H. Williamson, The Crawling Peg. (Dec. 1965)
* 51. Pieter Lieftinck, External Debt and Debt-Bearing Capacity of Developing Countries. (March 1966)
* 52. Raymond F. Mikesell, Public Foreign Capital for Private Enterprise in Developing Countries. (April 1966)
* 53. Milton Gilbert, Problems of the International Monetary System. (April 1966)
* 54. Robert V. Roosa and Fred Hirsch, Reserves, Reserve Currencies, and Vehicle Currencies: An Argument. (May 1966)
* 55. Robert Triffin, The Balance of Payments and the Foreign Investment Position of the United States. (Sept. 1966)
* 56. John Parke Young, United States Gold Policy: The Case for Change. (Oct. 1966)

PRINCETON STUDIES IN INTERNATIONAL FINANCE

†No. 1. Friedrich A. and Vera C. Lutz, Monetary and Foreign Exchange Policy in Italy. (Jan. 1950)
† 2. Eugene A. Schlesinger, Multiple Exchange Rates and Economic Development. (May 1952)
† 3. Arthur I. Bloomfield, Speculative and Flight Movements of Capital in Postwar International Finance. (Feb. 1954)
† 4. Merlyn N. Trued and Raymond F. Mikesell, Postwar Bilateral Payments Agreements. (April 1955)
† 5. Derek Curtis Bok, The First Three Years of the Schuman Plan. (Dec. 1955)

† 6. James E. Meade, Negotiations for Benelux: An Annotated Chronicle, 1943-1956. (March 1957)
† 7. H. H. Liesner, The Import Dependence of Britain and Western Germany: A Comparative Study. (Dec. 1957)
† 8. Raymond F. Mikesell and Jack N. Behrman, Financing Free World Trade with the Sino-Soviet Bloc. (Sept. 1958)
† 9. Marina von Neumann Whitman, The United States Investment Guaranty Program and Private Foreign Investment. (Dec. 1959)
† 10. Peter B. Kenen, Reserve-Asset Preferences of Central Banks and Stability of the Gold-Exchange Standard. (June 1963)
* 11. Arthur I. Bloomfield, Short-Term Capital Movements under the Pre-1914 Gold Standard. (July 1963)
* 12. Robert Triffin, The Evolution of the International Monetary System: Historical Reappraisal and Future Perspectives. (June 1964)
* 13. Robert Z. Aliber, The Management of the Dollar in International Finance. (June 1964)
* 14. Weir M. Brown, The External Liquidity of an Advanced Country. (Oct. 1964)
* 15. E. Ray Canterbery, Foreign Exchange, Capital Flows, and Monetary Policy. (June 1965)
* 16. Ronald I. McKinnon and Wallace E. Oates, The Implications of International Economic Integration for Monetary, Fiscal, and Exchange-Rate Policy. (March 1966)
* 17. Egon Sohmen, The Theory of Forward Exchange. (Aug. 1966)
* 18. Benjamin J. Cohen, Adjustment Costs and the Distribution of New Reserves. (Oct. 1966)

SPECIAL PAPERS IN INTERNATIONAL ECONOMICS

*No. 1. Gottfried Haberler, A Survey of International Trade Theory. (Sept. 1955; Revised edition, July 1961)
† 2. Oskar Morgenstern, The Validity of International Gold Movement Statistics. (Nov. 1955)
* 3. Fritz Machlup, Plans for Reform of the International Monetary System. (Apr. 1962; Revised edition, March 1964)
† 4. Egon Sohmen, International Monetary Problems and the Foreign Exchanges. (April 1963)
† 5. Walther Lederer, The Balance on Foreign Transactions: Problems of Definition and Measurement. (Sept. 1963)
* 6. George N. Halm, The "Band" Proposal: The Limits of Permissible Exchange Rate Variations. (Feb. 1965)
* 7. W. M. Corden, Recent Developments in the Theory of International Trade. (March 1965)

REPRINTS IN INTERNATIONAL FINANCE

* 1. Fritz Machlup, The Cloakroom Rule of International Reserves: Reserve Creation and Resources Transfer. [Reprinted from *Quarterly Journal of Economics*, Vol. LXXIX (Aug. 1965)]
† 2. Fritz Machlup, Real Adjustment, Compensatory Corrections, and Foreign Financing of Imbalances in International Payment. [Reprinted from Robert E. Baldwin et al., *Trade, Growth, and the Balance of Payments* (Chicago: Rand McNally and Amsterdam: North-Holland Publishing Co., 1965)]

* 3. Fritz Machlup, International Monetary Systems and the Free Market Economy. [Reprinted from *International Payments Problems: A Symposium* (Washington, D.C.; American Enterprise Institute, 1966)]

* 4. Fritz Machlup, World Monetary Debate—Bases for Agreement. [Reprinted from *The Banker*, Vol. 116 (Sept. 1966)]

* 5. Fritz Machlup, The Need for Monetary Reserves. [Reprinted from Banca Nazionale del Lavoro *Quarterly Review*, Vol. 77 (Sept. 1966)]

SEPARATE PUBLICATIONS

† (1) Klaus Knorr and Gardner Patterson (editors), A Critique of the Randall Commission Report. (1954)

† (2) Gardner Patterson and Edgar S. Furniss Jr. (editors), NATO: A Critical Appraisal. (1957)

* (3) Fritz Machlup and Burton G. Malkiel (editors), International Monetary Arrangements: The Problem of Choice. Report on the Deliberations of an International Study Group of 32 Economists. (Aug. 1964)

$1.00